Earth Day

Keeping Our Planet Clean

Elaine Landau

Enslow Publishers, Inc.

40 Industrial Road	PO Box 38
Box 398	Aldershot
Berkeley Heights, NJ 07922	Hants GU12 6BP
USA	UK

http://www.cnslow.com

For the Gorgeous Garmizo Girls!

Library of Congress Cataloging-in-Publication Data

Landau, Elaine.
  Earth Day—keeping our planet clean / Elaine Landau.
    p. cm. — (Finding out about holidays)
Includes bibliographical references and index.
Summary: Discusses the origins of Earth Day, its history, and how it is
observed in the United States today.
  ISBN 0-7660-1778-8
  1 Earth Day—Juvenile literature. 2. Environmentalism—United
States—Juvenile literature. 3. Environmental protection—United
States—Juvenile literature. [1. Earth Day. 2. Environmental protection.
3. Holidays.] I. Title. II. Series.
GE195.5 .L36 2002
333.7—dc21   2001003678

Printed in the United States of America

10 9 8 7 6 5 4 3 2 1

To Our Readers: We have done our best to make sure that all Internet addresses in this book were active and appropriate when we went to press. However, the author and publisher have no control over and assume no liability for the material available on those Internet sites or on other Web sites they may link to. Any comments or suggestions can be sent by e-mail to comments@enslow.com or to the address on the back cover.

Photo Credits: Bernard Gotfryd/Hulton/Archive by Getty Images, pp. 4, 36; Cheryl Wells, p. 43 (all); © Corel Corporation, pp. 6, 11, 12, 17, 18, 19, 25, 26 (inset), 27, 35, 44, 45, 46, 47, 48; Crady Von Pawlak/Hulton/Archive by Getty Images, p. 8; Dan Coleman/Hulton/Archive by Getty Images, p. 28; Díamar Interactive Corp., p. 22; Enslow Publishers, Inc., pp. 30, 40; Hemera Technologies, Inc., pp. 9 (both), 15 (all), 23 (inset), 38 (both), 39, 41; Herb Noseworth/Hulton/Archive by Getty Images, p. 10; http://www.earthdaybags.org/pics/01/nipher.htm, p. 29; Hulton/Archive by Getty Images, pp. 13, 16, 20; Images © 1995 Photo Disc, Inc., p. 5; Jeff Greenber/Hulton/Archive by Getty Images, p. 7; National Aeronautics and Space Administration, p. 21; Neil Strassberg/Hulton/Archive by Getty Images, p. 24; Ron Sachs/Hulton/Archive by Getty Images, p. 26 (large photo); Skjold Photographs, pp.i, ii, iii, 14, 31, 33, 47; United States Department of Agriculture, pp. 23 (large photo), 32, 34, 37.

Cover Photos: David Porter/Index Stock (large photo); Skjold Photographs (top inset), © Corel Corporation (middle inset), United States Department of Agriculture (bottom inset).

CONTENTS

Keeping our planet a clean, safe place to live is very important.

CHAPTER 1

Seeing Green

We live on the planet Earth. It is the only planet that has people living on it. It is also the only planet with animals, trees, and flowers. That makes it a special place. But what if Earth were a perfect place?

What if Earth were a place that was always clean and green? There would be fresh air everywhere. Clean water would flow in our rivers. Everyone would have a garden, or at least live near a park.

Trees would line our streets. They would shade our homes and schools. There would be

large open areas, too. People would live close to trees, mountains, oceans, and living things.

Sadly, Earth is not that way. There is a reason for that. We are not taking care of the environment (our natural surroundings). Factories and cars release dangerous fumes (smoke or gases) into the air. In some cities, the air is not safe for people to breathe.

Factories often release fumes (smoke or dangerous gases) into the air we breathe.

Garbage is being dumped into our water. This kills fish and other living things. It also makes many places unsafe for swimming. Garbage dumps across America are overflowing. Cities, businesses, and people create tons of trash.

Such damage to Earth is known as pollution. But it does not just happen in cities. Farmers put chemicals called pesticides on their crops. The pesticides kill bugs that harm crops. But they also kill wildlife and are dangerous for people to breathe.

Sometimes farmers put pesticides on their crops to kill bugs that might harm the plants. These chemicals can be dangerous for people.

Forests are disappearing. They are being cut down for wood or to make room to build. Often, forest animals lose their homes. Earth has become less green. It has also become less clean and less beautiful.

Many of our forests are disappearing. They are being cut down for wood or to make room to build.

Some people are trying to change that. There is a special day to honor and protect our planet. It is known as Earth Day.

Earth Day is held every year on April 22. It is a day to think about the environment. There are meetings, fairs, and rallies. People plan ways to make things better. They clean up lakes and rivers. Trees and gardens are planted. Many people of all ages take part. That is because Earth belongs to all of us. We are all responsible for it.

Some people plant gardens on Earth Day. This is one way for us to make our surroundings more beautiful.

It is important to keep wide-open spaces like this corn field clean and protected.

CHAPTER 2
Through the Years

American Indians were the first people here. They took good care of the land and used it wisely. They did not pollute the land or the streams. They did not waste food, water, or trees. American Indians did not think that the land belonged to the people. They said that the people belonged to the Earth.

There was not always an Earth Day. We did not always need one. The American Indians were the first people here. They took care of the land and used it wisely.

In the 1600s, people from Europe arrived. Things began to change. In time, fields gave way to farms, towns, and cities. Businesses opened and factories were built.

The population grew, too. More people needed more things. So businesses produced more goods. Cars and buses replaced wagons pulled by horses. There were superhighways instead of dirt roads. These changes were known

EXIT 3B
Grand Ave
SECOND RIGHT

The fumes from cars
on our roads create a
lot of air pollution.

as progress. Progress was supposed to be a good thing. In some ways, it was. But it was not always good for the air, land, and water.

Yet, few people thought about this. Earth's gifts seemed endless. But we learned that they were not. By the early 1960s, our air, land, and water were badly polluted.

Gaylord Nelson was governor of the state of Wisconsin. He saw the problem and he wanted to change things. So he went on a speaking tour across America. He visited more than twenty-five states. He asked people to try to clean up the environment.

Nelson thought that having an Earth Day would be a good start. He knew that college students sometimes shared ideas in a special way. They held "teach-ins." At these meetings, the students talked about problems. They

Gaylord Nelson was governor of the state of Wisconsin. He asked people to clean up our surroundings.

Recycling is one way that we can all reduce the amount of garbage that we produce.

worked on ways to change things. Nelson wanted to hold a huge teach-in for Earth Day.

Gaylord Nelson knew he could not plan Earth Day alone. He asked a college student to help him. That student's name was Dennis Hayes. Like Nelson, Hayes cared about the environment. A special office was set up in

Washington, D.C., to plan Earth Day. Other people came there to help.

The first Earth Day was held on April 22, 1970. Twenty million Americans took part. They were from towns and cities all over the United States. More than two thousand colleges throughout the United States held Earth Day events.

In New York City, several streets were closed to cars. The space was used for an Earth Day fair. Students in Omaha, Nebraska, wore gas masks that day. They wanted to make people more aware of air pollution.

In Florida, people marched outside a power company. They brought along twenty pounds of dead fish. The power company had been releasing very hot water

If we pollute our rivers and oceans, the fish that live in those waters will die.

Workers sort out mixed waste into piles of plastic, glass, aluminum, and cardboard for recycling.

into the bay. This caused many fish to die. The Earth Day marchers hoped to stop this.

A goat took part in Earth Day in Centralia, Washington. The goat was put out on a lawn. It had a sign on it that said: "I eat garbage—what do you do for the environment?"

The first Earth Day was a huge success and there were many neighborhood cleanups. People picked trash and litter out of rivers. They planted community gardens in empty lots. Thousands of Americans promised to make Earth a cleaner planet.

Earth Day changed the way we look at our environment. It made people more aware of the problems. Earth Day also made

Cleaning up the environment helps to keep the animals that live in it healthy.

Soon, the government passed laws to help protect the air and water from pollution.

government officials more aware of the need for changes.

Soon, some valuable changes occurred. The Environmental Protection Agency was established. It is a government agency that helps to keep the environment safe. The Clean Air Act and Clean Water Acts were also passed. These laws protect the environment, too. The Endangered Species Act was passed as well. This law protects animals. Many animals had become extinct (died out). They had been killed by hunters or died when their homes were destroyed. Other animals were close to dying out.

Earth Day 1970 became an important day in our nation's history. It was the birth of the modern environmental movement. This united Americans in protecting the planet.

Today, we have many laws that protect animals from losing their homes and being killed by hunters.

Garbage dumps all over the country, like this one in New York, are piled high with unwanted waste.

CHAPTER 3

More Recently

Our planet is sick because we have not taken good care of it. But Earth Day and every day, we work to make it better. Together, we can work to stop pollution. We can save wildlife. We can protect our forests.

At first, Earth Day did not take place every year. In fact, the next Earth Day after the first celebration in 1970 was twenty years later, in 1990.

But people had not forgotten that special day. Many still hoped to save the planet. They formed groups to protect the environment. Some groups worked on stopping pollution. Others worked to save wildlife. Still others tried to protect the forests.

Over time, they each had some success. However, these environmental groups felt we needed another Earth Day. Some group leaders met with Dennis Hayes. They wanted him to plan an Earth Day for 1990.

Hayes was no longer a student. Now he was a lawyer. But he still wanted to help. He left his job for a while. He needed time to work on this project.

Hayes' work paid off. Earth Day 1990 was a worldwide event. Two hundred million people in 141 countries took part. This was important. No one country can protect Earth by itself. People from around the globe have to help. Different countries need to work together.

On Earth Day 1990, millions of trees were planted in South America. In Japan, there were meetings about pollution. Canadians declared war on litter. Small armies of people took part in cleanups.

Everyone can help take care of the Earth. Planting trees and gardens is one way to do this.

Even kids can do their part to keep trees growing where they live.

Groups in the United States were especially busy. There were both land and river cleanups. Acres of trees were planted. Many towns held Earth Day fairs. People at these events served delicious organic foods. These are foods grown without the use of pesticides.

After 1990, things changed. Earth Day was held every year. This has been good for the environment. People need to remember our planet. Earth deserves its own day.

Gaylord Nelson continued to help. He became known as the Father of Earth Day. In 1995, Nelson was awarded the Presidential Medal of Freedom. This is one of our nation's highest honors.

Every Earth Day has been important. But Earth Day 2000 was extra special. That was Earth Day's thirtieth birthday. It was also the first Earth Day of the twenty-first century. Over 500 million people from many different countries took part.

The United Nations

Organic foods are grown without using any chemicals that might be harmful to the people who eat those foods.

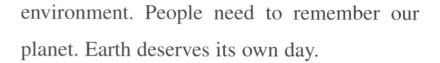

(UN) in New York City had an Earth Day celebration, too. The United Nations is a group of people from almost all of the world's free countries. The UN works for world peace. One child from every country in the United Nations took part in the celebration. The children dressed in costumes from their homelands. Each

planted an olive tree, a symbol of peace, in the UN's garden. During the ceremony, 189 white pigeons were set free. There are 189 countries in the UN.

Many Earth Day events were held in other parts of the United States. There was an Earth Day fair in Washington, D.C. Movie stars and

People helped to clean streams and lakes so that animals such as the whooping crane could return to their homes.

To celebrate Earth Day in 2000, white pigeons were set free as part of a special ceremony at the United Nations in New York.

elected officials spoke to the crowd. They urged people to care for the environment. Thousands of people listened and applauded.

In Louisville, Kentucky, more than thirty thousand trees were planted. An Earth Day hike was held in Eugene, Oregon. The hikers

enjoyed being in the wilderness. They also talked about ways to protect it.

Scuba divers were active, too. They had their own Earth Day 2000 event. It was called "Dive into Earth Day!" The divers cleaned up beaches. They also did underwater cleanups. More than twenty-five hundred divers helped. They picked up about thirty-five thousand pounds of trash.

Earth Day is not a national holiday. Each state decides for itself how to celebrate. Banks and businesses do not close. Mail is delivered that day. But it is still an important day. Earth Day is a reminder that we must respect and protect our surroundings.

Scuba divers cleaned up beaches and did underwater cleanups for Earth Day in 2000.

These recycling bins help to keep different kinds of trash separated.

CHAPTER 4

Earth Day at School

EARTH DAY PROJECTS ON THE INTERNET

★

Some students like those from Nipher Middle School in Missouri, have put their Earth Day artwork on the Internet. For more information on this fun Web site, see Internet Addresses on page 47.

Young people are busy on Earth Day. Thousands of students from all over the United States take part in the "Earth Day Groceries Project." Students draw pictures about Earth on large brown paper bags. Some people write Earth Day messages on the bags, too.

The bags are put in stores on Earth Day. When people buy something, it is put in one of the bags. This helps people to think about the environment. It is a fun way to spread the word.

Students do other things, too. In one Tennessee school, each student brought in a

If everyone pitches in and recycles, we can reuse much of the glass, plastic, and aluminum the things we buy come packaged in.

nickel. The money was used to buy a tree that the students planted on Earth Day.

Many young people work on recycling projects. Through recycling, old items are reused and made into new things. This creates less waste.

For Earth Day some students in Louisiana recycled newspapers. They collected the newspapers and took them to local recycling centers. The students saw that their work counted. Paper is made from trees. Recycling newspapers saves trees. Every nine grocery bags that the students filled with newspapers equaled one tree saved.

Other students recycled, too. They put on Earth Day fashion shows by wearing "recycled" fashions. Their outfits looked new, but they were made out of old clothes.

These students are recycling paper and cardboard.

Recycling was part of some Earth Day art shows, too. Students made recycled sculptures. They used old toys and common household items to make "Earth-Smart" art.

In many schools, students find ways to save energy. This helps the environment. Oil and gas are used for energy. These things come

Paper is usually made from trees, but a fast-growing plant called _kenaf_ could be used instead of wood for paper-making.

from deep within our planet. But they will not last forever. We need to conserve or save oil and gas. Using less energy also keeps the air cleaner.

Some California students formed energy patrols. The patrols shut off the lights when classes leave the room. This saves energy during lunch and recess periods. The patrols

These recycling bins at the side of the road are a reminder to us all to do our part to keep our Earth clean.

Students sometimes plant gardens on Earth Day.

also make "Save Energy" signs. They put these next to all the light switches. The idea is to tell others to use energy wisely.

Schools do other things for Earth Day as well. Sometimes they plant gardens.

Sometimes they put on Earth Day plays. They have Earth Day fairs and poster contests. At times, students dress for Earth Day. Their schools may ask them to wear a special T-shirt that makes people think about Earth Day. The shirt can have a picture of Earth on it, or it can show an endangered animal. Some shirts have Earth Day messages printed on them.

Earth's resources are limited, but the ways we can protect the planet are not. Many schools are proving this is true.

Keeping our streams clean is an important part of Earth Day.

The first Earth Day festival took place in New York City in the early 1970s.

CHAPTER 5

What You Can Do

Why not make every day Earth Day? Try some of these Earth-saving tips:

✔ Take showers instead of baths. Showers use less water.

✔ When brushing your teeth, do not let the water run. This wastes a great deal of water.

✔ Shut all faucets tightly. Leaky faucets waste water.

✔ When leaving a room, remember to turn off the lights, television, and computer. This saves electricity.

A PROBLEM WITH PLASTIC

Petroleum-based plastic products now take up about 25 percent of the volume of landfills. Instead of using petroleum-based plastics, we can use plastic bags and wraps made from an earth-friendly starch-polyester material. Shown below are forks, knives, and spoons made from the starch-polyester material.

Do not let the water run while you brush your teeth. This wastes a lot of water.

✔ Avoid single-serving containers. The packages they come in create extra, unneeded garbage. Some toys have too much packaging, as well. This is done to make the toy look better. It is not better for the planet, however. It does not make the toy any more fun to play with, either. Think of the environment when you shop. Buy "Earth-Smart" things that do not come in too much packaging.

✔ Recycle what you have outgrown. Many charities accept old clothing. Hospitals and daycare centers take old toys. Libraries often accept used books. They sell them at book sales. That means more money for new books. It also means less garbage.

✔ Do you bring lunch to school? Try carrying it in a reusable bag. Paper bags increase waste. Try to reuse grocery bags from stores, or take a cloth tote bag with you instead. It can be used again and again.

✔ Do not always ask for a ride. Cars cause air pollution. Bicycles do not. They do not give off fumes. Neither do your feet. Think twice when you are going somewhere. Can riding a bike or walking get you there? Those would be better choices for the environment.

✔ Write, write, write. Let people know how you feel about the environment. Put your

If you bring your lunch to school, use a reusable bag instead of a paper one.

Cars cause air pollution.
Bicycles do not.

thoughts in a letter. Try writing to your local newspaper. Your letter might be printed. Write to elected officials, too. Your librarian can help you find the addresses.

These are just a few of the things you can do to help the planet. Can you think of others? If so, try them. Earth is the only home we have. We need to take care of it on Earth Day and every day.

If you choose to bike or skate, make sure to wear a helmet!

Earth Day Project

★

Stone Paperweight

You can make stone paperweights for your friends and family. If you wrap them as gifts, remember to use recycled paper. The stones also make great room decorations. They are fun to collect and trade, too. You will need:

✔ **a smooth stone (any shape)**

✔ **a colored pencil**

✔ **a paintbrush**

✔ **poster paints**

1. Wash the stone well. Let it dry for at least a day.

2. Use the colored pencil to draw something on the stone. You can create a nature scene or an animal. You might prefer to just make a design. You can erase any mistakes if you use a pencil.

3. With the paintbrush and the poster paints, paint over what you have drawn.

4. Let the stone dry overnight.

*Safety Note: Be sure to ask for help from an adult, if needed, to complete this project.

Earth Day Project

Ready to start!

Having fun painting!

Paperweights finished!

Words to Know
★

conserve—To protect or use carefully.

endangered—At risk of dying out and disappearing completely.

environment—Our natural surroundings.

extinct—An animal or plant that no longer exists.

litter—Trash.

natural resources—Anything of value found in nature, such as water, soil, forests, and wildlife.

organic foods—Foods grown without the use of chemicals.

pesticides—Chemicals that kill insects in crops.

Words to Know

★

pollution—Damage to Earth's land, air, or water.

Presidential Medal of Freedom—The highest honor that can be awarded to someone who is not in the United States military.

recycle—To reuse something.

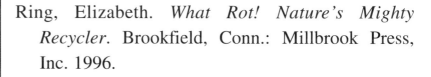

Reading About

★

Arnosky, Jim. *Crinkleroot's Guide to Knowing Animal Habitats*. New York: Simon & Schuster, 1997.

Hirschi, Ron. *Save Our Wetlands*. New York: Delacorte, 1994.

Ring, Elizabeth. *What Rot! Nature's Mighty Recycler*. Brookfield, Conn.: Millbrook Press, Inc. 1996.

Ross, Kathy. *Every Day Is Earth Day: A Craft Book*. Brookfield, Conn.: Millbrook Press, Inc., 1995.

Royston, Angela. *Recycling*. Orlando, Fla.: Raintree Steck-Vaughn Publishers, 1999.

Staub, Frank S. *America's Forests*. Minneapolis, Minn.: Carolrhoda, 1999.

Internet Addresses

★

EARTH DAY BAGS
<http://www.earthdaybags.org>

EPA FOR KIDS
<http://www.epa.gov/kids>

KIDS DOMAIN EARTH DAY
<http://www.kidsdomain.com/holiday/earthday>

PLANET PALS
<http://www.planetpals.com>

Index

★